A DAY IN THE LIFE OF A SCIENTIST

an imprint of mehta publishers

MEHTA publishers

A Day in the Life of a Scientist

ISBN: 978-93-86096-12-8

Published by: Mehta Publishers
The story typeface is KB Drunk Tank

Mehta House, A-16, Naraina Phase II,
New Delhi-110028 (India)
E-mail: info@mehtapublishers.com

Printed in India by Mehta Offset Pvt. Ltd.

First Edition

This Book Belongs To

Aceman Pharmaceuticals Ltd

Julie and Tom were waiting in the parking lot for Dr. Lucy Morgan. She was a scientist in Aceman Pharmaceuticals ltd. It was a Friday and the children were spending an entire day with her for a class project.

"Hello Lucy", they said with a bright smile. As Dr. Lucy Morgan walked towards them, she noticed Julie nudging Tom. She looked at the giggling children in mock anger and said, "Has Tom been telling you that I am Dr. Evil and I am working on a serum to create super humans?"

Julie smiled nervously. Lucy laughed loudly and hugged Tom, her young nephew.

"Aunt Lucy, do you reach office early everyday?" Tom enquired as they passed through the security check near the main door.

"I reach office at seven o'clock in the morning. It gives me a head start. I get time to check my emails and plan the tasks for my team. Let's go inside and I will show you around," replied Dr. Lucy.

Julie and Tom followed Dr. Lucy inside the building. The reception and the lobby were brightly lit. A few people were sitting on the couches in the lobby, reading magazines and articles. They saw few scientists rushing to reach their office on time.

"We have a tightly planned schedule and everything needs to be done on time," explained Dr. Lucy. Then they took the elevator to the third floor to reach her office.

After entering her office, Dr. Lucy picked up a white lab coat and a pair of glasses.

"Why do you need those?" Julie asked curiously.

"The lab coat prevents the clothes from getting stained. It also offers protection from burns due to accidents. These safety glasses protect my eyes from chemical fumes."

"Can we get one of those," asked Tom.

Dr. Lucy gave them white lab coats and glasses but they were too large for them.

Then they began the tour of other offices in the building and soon walked into a large discussion room.

"This is the conference room where the head of our department briefs us about the forthcoming projects. They also guides the junior researchers and track the progress of current projects," explained Dr. Lucy.

Soon the conference room filled up with scientists. Dr. Stevens, the head of the department reviewed the progress of all the scientists. He offered some suggestions to the

new interns and assigned them new projects. Soon everyone left the conference room. Dr Stevens walked up to Tom and asked, "So you are Lucy's nephew. I hope you children enjoy the tour around the facility."

"Yes Sir! I want to become a scientist." Tom replied with excitement. Dr. Stevens wished them good luck and went back to his office.

Dr. Lucy then took them to the lab. "This is so cool!" exclaimed Julie excitedly as soon as they entered the lab.

Dr. Lucy pointed to the apparatus and said, "My team and I are testing a new drug."

"How are new medicines made?" enquired Julie

"Creating a new medicine is a long and rigorous process and can take several years. Most medicines used today are manufactured through chemical processes. We might even test 5,000 or more different chemicals to identify the one

that is effective against the disease. We then test it on animals and and if successful then on humans to check for any possible side effects. The drug is finally approved for commercial use after undergoing several trails."

Tom who loved all sorts of machines and equipment asked curiously, "What are all these instruments for?"

"This is a microscope. We use it to observe very small organisms and the effect of chemical compounds on these organisms."

Dr. Lucy, Julie and Tom then walk towards the end of the lab. The children were very quiet, as they don't want to disturb the researchers who are working with concentration. At the end of the hall a researcher was typing data into a computer.

"The information from the observations and tests are stored here. Dr. Brenda evaluates their progress and compiles their progress report. She briefs Dr. Stevens and me on the progress made by each team. This information about the project is available to all the project members."

"It is wonderful to see new faces today, Lucy. Are they joining the team?" joked Dr. Brenda.

"I would love to join this place." Tom replied with a broad smile.

Dr. Lucy then informed Dr. Brenda. "Brenda, please remind the team that Dr. McLean's conference is scheduled at 3 PM tomorrow. Everyone should reach the conference hall in time."

Dr. Brenda looked towards the scientists and replied, "They are all very excited about his visit. They won't miss it for anything."

Dr. Lucy then look at her watch and said. "It's time for me to catch up with my assistants and discuss the progress on an experiment."

Tom and Julie waved good-bye to Brenda and walked with Dr. Lucy to her office.

For the next hour or so, Dr. Lucy and her assistants discussed an experiment, which was not going as well as they hoped. Dr. Lucy offered a few possible solutions, which encouraged her assistants. They took notes and made a few diagrams, which Dr. Lucy corrected.

After they had left, Dr. Lucy addressed the children. "As a scientist it is easy to get discouraged as there are a lot of failed attempts before you actually get a positive result. It helps to think of the lives of people who would benefit from our research. That helps us to move forward with enthusiasm."

Julie and Tom were impressed with Dr. Lucy. "Being a scientist isn't easy at all," said Tom, who was a feeling a little tired now.

They laughed.

"Yes, it is not easy, but a successful experiment rejuvenates and motivates us all," replied Dr. Lucy.

Just then Dr. Brenda peeked inside Dr.Lucys cabin and said. "I need to discuss the re-agents and items we need for the experiment C-345, which is due to start next week."

Dr. Lucy nodded for Dr. Brenda to come in while she continued explaining to the kids. "Other than researching and mentoring, I also need to plan for experiments. Once a lab manager requests for an experiment, I need to ensure that my team gets all the experimental components like instruments, chemicals and re-agents."

Julie and Tom nodded seriously.

The telephone rang. It was Dr. Stevens. "I need to meet Dr. Stevens right away, Brenda. Could you please get Julie and Tom lunch and then show them our library, said Dr. Lucy.

Lunch and then library! exclaimed Tom wide-eyed. Suddenly he wasn't tired anymore.

Dr Brenda took the children for lunch to the canteen and then proceeded to the library.

"All the scientists need to constantly refer to books and research papers. Some of them are writing research papers. A well-stocked library is essential for their research and studies. They spend a lot of time in the library. Our library has more than 10,000 books. We also have lot of books in digital format, which are stored in the computers. Besides you can access several articles and books on the internet." explained Dr. Brenda as they entered the library.

Tom and Julie were impressed.

The scientists were curious about Tom and Julie's visit. They enquired about their school assignment. Soon everyone gathered around Tom and Julie. They eagerly shared their experiences with them and answered all their queries. Tom and Julie got busy taking notes.

Suddenly Dr. Brenda's phone began to beep. She answered her phone and said, "Let's go to Lucy's office. She is back."

Dr. Brenda escorted them to Dr. Lucy's office, and after a brief discussion about the chemicals she left. The children then narrated their experiences of interacting with various scientists and their work. "So you found a lot about the work we do here?" asked Dr. Lucy.

"Yes! What time do you go home?" asked Julie

"Most of the days we leave at six but sometimes we stay back for longer hours if we have an important experiment to finish. Sometimes there are symposiums or conferences that extend late into the evening. In case the project is getting close to the deadline, we work on holidays as well."

The children were surprised. "Don't you get bored?"

Dr. Lucy showed them a picture album. "We don't work hard all the time. The company gives us a handsome salary and other perks. These pictures are from a company-sponsored vacation in the Caribbean Islands. My team had a lot of fun and we were fully recharged after a long vacation."

Dr. Lucy looked at the watch. "It is 5:00pm. Time for you to go home."

Dr. Lucy, Julie and Tom had reached the parking lot when Julie asked, "Why did you pick this profession Dr. Lucy?"

Dr. Lucy spoke with a smile, "I was waiting for that question. I want to create drugs, which cure the disease, and help mankind."

Tom and Julie were impressed with Dr. Lucy's dedication. The children realized that the life of a scientist is tough. Being a scientist requires patience, dedication and hard work.

Dr. Lucy drove them back to their home in her car. They waved Dr. Lucy goodbye and rushed back to their home to finish their class assignment.

Titles of This Series

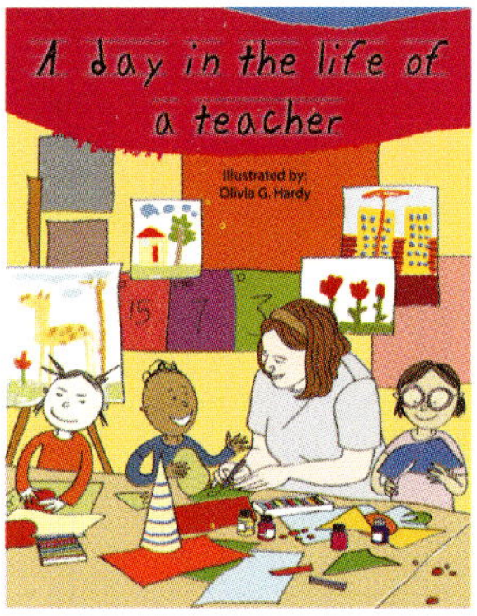